WEST CHICAGO PUBLIC LIBRARY DISTRICT
3 6653 00254 7580
P9-CFI-852

West Chicago Public Library District
118 West Washington
West Chicago, IL 60185-2803
Phone # (630) 231-1552
Fax # (630) 231-1709

2/10

Written and Illustrated by Caroline Arnold

A Day and Night on the PRAIRIE

PICTURE WINDOW BOOKS
a capstone imprint

6:00 A.M.

Wee-o! Wee-o! call the prairie dogs.

It is a cool spring morning on the prairie. One by one the prairie dogs pop out of their holes and look for fresh grass to eat. If they see a predator, they will dash back into their burrows.

Prairie dogs live in groups called towns. Some towns are home to hundreds of prairie dogs.

The pronghorn antelope are hungry too. They snip off leaves and flowers with sharp front teeth. If any pronghorn senses danger, it will raise the hairs on its rump and alert the rest of the herd. Then all the animals will race across the prairie to safety.

9:00 A.M.

A male meadowlark sings. His mate snaps up spiders and insects with her long bill. She will take them back to her nest to feed her hungry chicks.

In a sunny spot nearby, a box turtle warms itself. Soon it will search for insects, worms, and berries to eat. If a large animal comes near, the box turtle will pull its head, tail, and legs into its hard shell. Even the sharp teeth of a fox or coyote cannot bite through it.

Box turtle shells are hinged on the bottom. They allow the turtles to pull in all their soft body parts and protect them from predators.

NOON

The day grows warmer. A hawk spreads its wings to catch a rising air current. It soars over the prairie, looking for rabbits, prairie dogs, and other small animals to eat. When the hawk spots its prey, it dives and grabs the prey with its sharp talons.

A bison herd moves across the prairie. Young bison stay close to their mothers. The bison bite off clumps of grass. They chew slowly, grinding the plants with their large back teeth.

Bison are the largest animals on the prairie. Females may weigh more than 1,000 pounds (454 kilograms). Males are often twice as heavy! A newborn bison calf weighs about 65 pounds (29 kg).

3:00 P.M.

All day long an orb-weaving spider sits in her web. She waits for a fly, bee, or grasshopper to get stuck in the silky threads. Once her prey is caught, the spider wraps it to eat later.

Nearby a garter snake slips through the grass. It flicks its forked tongue while hunting for toads, worms, and other small animals. It follows their smell. If the sun becomes too hot, the garter snake will look for a shady spot to stay cool.

Snakes that live on the prairie include garter snakes, king snakes, ringneck snakes, and rattlesnakes.

9:00 P.M.

Ribbit! Ribbit! Frogs croak at the edge of a small pond. Bats swoop over the dark water and catch moths and mosquitoes. A family of skunks stops for a drink.

A thirsty fox waits until the skunks have gone before coming to the pond. It does not want to get sprayed by them. After drinking, the fox hunts for mice and small animals. It may eat berries and seeds too.

If a skunk meets a predator and cannot escape, it will spray the predator with a smelly liquid. The liquid comes from glands on the skunk's rear end.

MIDNIGHT

All through the night, mice scurry across the prairie. They stuff seeds, nuts, and insects into their cheek pouches. They will eat the food later, when they are safe in their burrows.

A fox listens for squeaks and rustles in the grass. It sniffs the air for animal scents. When the fox finds its prey, it pounces and grabs the animal with its teeth.

Pocket mice get their name from the large outside pouches, or "pockets," in their cheeks.

A bobcat creeps on silent paws. Its spotted fur blends into the shadows. It finds a vole busy collecting seeds. The vole does not see or hear the bobcat. The bobcat pounces!

A badger is hunting too. It smells a mouse and follows it to a hole. Quickly the badger digs into the dirt with its powerful claws and captures the mouse.

A badger's curved claws, which grow up to 2 inches (5 centimeters) long, are ideal for digging.

6:00 A.M.

The sky grows light, and a coyote finishes an early morning hunt. Bats fly back to their roosts, bobcats curl up for a long nap, and badgers go into their dens. It is time for daytime animals to wake up. Birds sing, bees buzz, and prairie dogs come out of their holes.

Every day and every night, animals find food, water, and safe places to rest on the prairie. It provides them with everything they need.

What Is a Prairie?

A prairie is a type of grassland. It has hot summers and cold winters.

Long ago the prairie in North America stretched for 1,000 miles (1,600 kilometers), from the Rocky Mountains to eastern Indiana, and from Saskatchewan, Canada, to Texas. Some of it still exists. But much of the North American prairie has been plowed to make way for farms and cities.

In the western part of the North American prairie lies the shortgrass prairie. Its plants grow to about 1.5 feet (0.5 meters) tall. In the eastern part lies the tallgrass prairie. Because more rain and snow fall in the east, tallgrass prairie plants grow tall. They reach heights of 5 feet (1.5 m) or more. In between lies the mixed-grass prairie.

Throughout the day and night, animals are busy on the prairie. Diurnal animals are active during the day. Nocturnal animals are active at night. Which animals in this book are diurnal? Which are nocturnal? Where do they live on the prairie?

Where Can You Find Grasslands?

About one-fourth of Earth's land is covered in grass. Grasslands are found on every continent except Antarctica. In North America they are called prairies. In South America they are called pampas. In Europe and Asia they are called steppes. In Africa they are called savannas. Grasslands closest to the equator are hot all year. Those that are farther from the equator, such as the prairies in North America, have hot summers and cold winters.

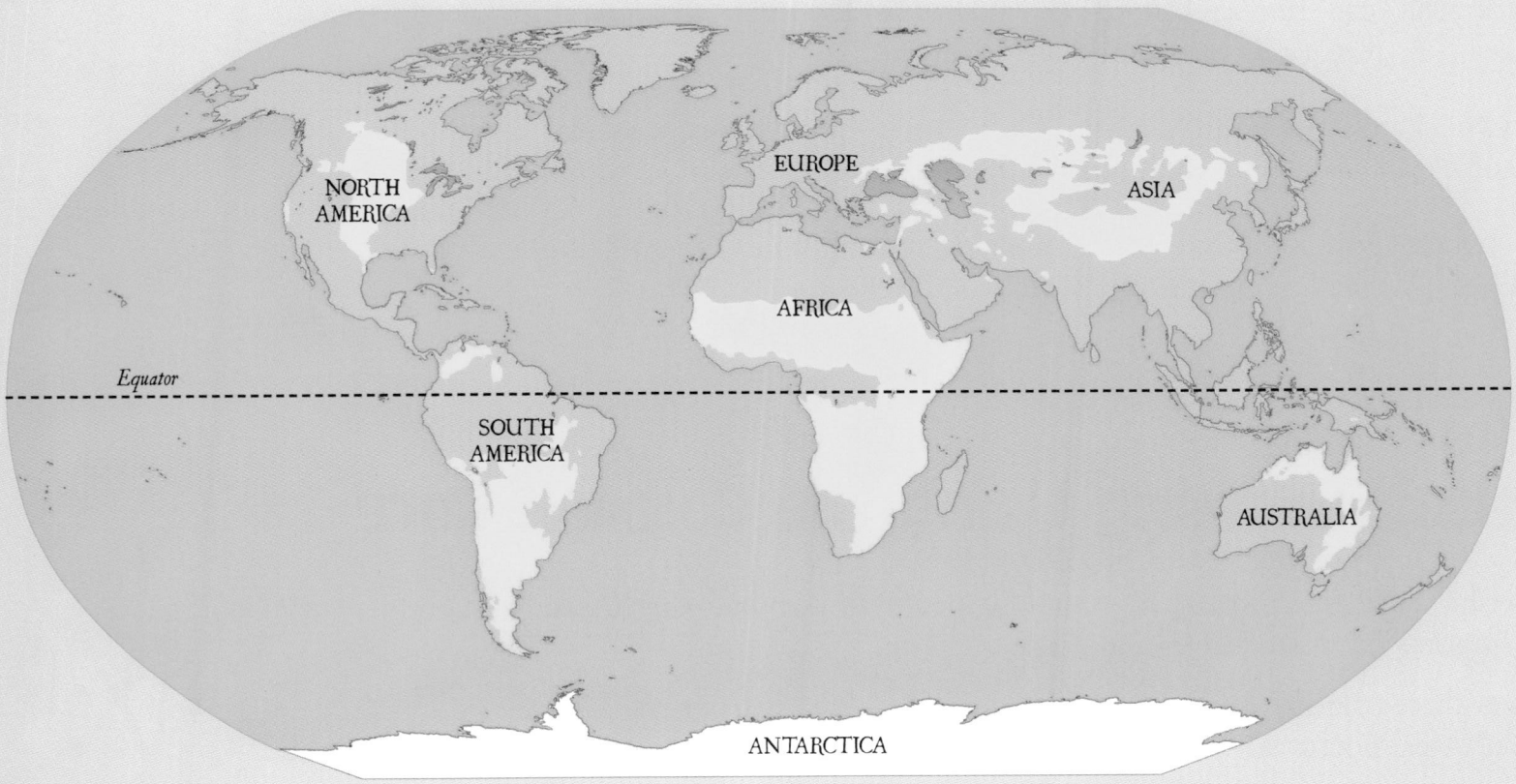

Grasslands

Fun Facts

- Pronghorn antelope have amazing eyesight. They can spot a moving object from 3 miles (4.8 km) away!
- Prairie dog burrows have rooms for sleeping, raising young prairie dogs, and storing food. Some even have bathrooms.
- When a meadowlark sees a predator, such as a snake, it freezes and lowers its head. It stays still until the predator is out of sight.
- When box turtles hatch from their eggs, they are about the size of quarters.
- Bison roll in the dust to escape from biting insects.
- A jackrabbit can run as fast as 40 miles (64 km) per hour. At top speed it can leap 15 feet (4.6 m) in a single bound.
- No two skunks are exactly alike. Each skunk has its own pattern of stripes. A skunk can shoot its spray up to 12 feet (3.7 m)!
- The bobcat gets its name from its short, stubby tail. The tail looks as if it has been "bobbed," or cut off.

Critical Thinking Using the Common Core

1. Describe how the passing of time is shown throughout this book. (Integration of Knowledge and Ideas)
2. Name three diurnal predators on the prairie and their prey. Then name three nocturnal predators and their prey. (Key Ideas and Details)

Glossary

burrow—a tunnel or hole in the ground made or used by an animal for shelter

current—the movement of air or water in a certain direction

diurnal—active during the day

equator—an imaginary line around the middle of Earth

gland—a cell or organ that makes natural chemical substances for use in the body or for discharge into the surroundings

habitat—the natural home or environment of an animal, plant, or other living thing

herd—a large group of animals that lives or moves together

nocturnal—active at night

predator—an animal that hunts other animals for food

prey—an animal hunted by another animal for food

roost—a place where birds and bats can sit and rest

talon—a long, sharp claw of a bird

Read More

Fredericks, Anthony D. *P Is for Prairie Dog: A Prairie Alphabet.* Ann Arbor, Mich.: Sleeping Bear Press, 2011.

Grucella, A. J. *Prairie Dogs in Danger.* Animals at Risk. New York: Gareth Stevens Publishing, 2014.

Rissman, Rebecca. *Living and Nonliving in the Grasslands.* Is It Living or Nonliving? Chicago: Capstone Raintree, 2013.

Root, Phyllis. *Plant a Pocket of Prairie.* Minneapolis: University of Minnesota Press, 2014.

Index

badgers, 17, 19
bats, 12, 19
birds, 4, 6, 10, 11, 19, 22
bison, 7, 22
bobcats, 16, 19, 22
coyotes, 5, 19
daytime, 2–10, 19, 20
foxes, 5, 12, 14
frogs, 12
grasslands, 20, 21
insects, 4, 5, 8, 12, 14, 19, 22
map, 21
mice, 12, 14, 17
nighttime, 11–19, 20
prairie dogs, 2, 6, 10, 11, 19, 22
pronghorn antelope, 3, 22
rabbits, 6, 10, 22
skunks, 12, 13, 22
snakes, 9, 22
spiders, 4, 8
turtles, 5, 22
voles, 11, 16

Internet Sites

FactHound offers a safe, fun way to find Internet sites related to this book. All of the sites on FactHound have been researched by our staff.

Here's all you do:

Visit *www.facthound.com*

Type in this code: 9781479560738

Special thanks to our adviser for his expertise:

Terry Flaherty, PhD, Professor of English
Minnesota State University, Mankato

Editor: Jill Kalz
Designer: Lori Bye
Art Director: Nathan Gassman
Production Specialist: Kathy McColley
The illustrations in this book were created with cut paper.
Design Elements: Shutterstock/Alfondo de Tomas (map), Alvaro Cabrera Jimenez

Picture Window Books are published by Capstone,
1710 Roe Crest Drive, North Mankato, Minnesota 56003
www.capstonepub.com

Copyright © 2015 by Caroline Arnold. All rights reserved. No part of this publication may be reproduced in whole or in part, or stored in a retrieval system, or transmitted in any form or by any means, electronic, mechanical, photocopying, recording, or otherwise, without written permission of the publisher.

Library of Congress Cataloging-in-Publication Data
Arnold, Caroline, author, illustrator.
A day and night on the prairie / written and illustrated by Caroline Arnold.
pages cm.—(Nonfiction picture books. Caroline Arnold's habitats)
Summary: "Highlights the activities of animals on the North American prairie during one average 24-hour period"—Provided by publisher.
Audience: K to grade 3.
Includes bibliographical references and index.
ISBN 978-1-4795-6073-8 (library binding)
ISBN 978-1-4795-6085-1 (paperback)
ISBN 978-1-4795-6145-2 (eBook PDF)
1. Grassland animals—Behavior—North America—Juvenile literature.
2. Grassland animals—North America—Juvenile literature. I. Title.
QL115.3.A77 2015
591.74097—dc23 2014025336

Look for all the books in the series:

Printed in the United States of America in North Mankato, Minnesota 092014 008482CGS15